Everything's Possible With Autism

My Epic Autism Journey and Easy

Ways You Can Overcome Your Child's

Obstacles with Autism

Austinn Weaver, B.A.

CONTENTS

Austinn Weaver

ACKNOWLEDGMENTS

I am really thankful to a few people who not only helped me write this book, but have shaped my life with all of the love and support; as they encouraged me every step of the way with my own Autism journey.

To my awesome parents, Lisa Darelli and Eric Weaver, your love, patience, and understanding have always been the foundation of my own strength. Thank you for always being by my side and for helping me throughout every challenge; especially with your selfless decisions and unwavering love.

To another amazing and special person in my life named Jessica Jacobsen, your presence in my life has been a gift beyond measure. Your understanding, empathy, and the belief you've shown me have made a profound difference along my Autism journey. I am always really thankful for your support, love, and compassion you've poured into my life.

My heart is filled with appreciation for all three of you who have been the biggest encouragement to my journey. All of your guidance, kindness, and support have always been invaluable.

Finally, I also want to thank the rest of my family members and friends for contributing, understanding, and accepting me with my own Autism. Thank you all for your love and support also!!

INTRODUCTION

Have you ever been wondered if it's possible for your child with Autism to live the life that both you and your child have been dreaming of? To answer that question, it is absolutely possible to make that dream come true; especially if you want your child to live the life like everyone else in this world.

My name is Austinn Weaver, and this book is a chronicle of my own epic Autism journey on how I had to deal with my own obstacles growing up, starting when I was diagnosed with Autism at age two and was nonverbal until age five. But my own epic journey with Autism is more than just a story; it's also to give you a brilliant idea on how you can help your child to beat the barriers of his or her own Autism. So, in this way, nothing stands in the way of beating the odds with Autism.

When you read on through my epic Autism journey, you will start to have an idea that *Everything's Possible With Autism*. It all just takes a matter of time, understanding, and patience to break down one barrier at a time for a child with Autism, as it just takes a special someone to believe in them. In fact, it even took all the extra help from both of my parents and my stepmom, who all believed in me to help me break down my own barriers with Autism; such barriers were being unable to speak until age five, spinning in circles, doing weird hand movements, talking to myself publicly, and being unable to focus in school to where was not able to succeed academically.

Research states that "According to the Centers for Disease Control and Prevention (CDC), approximately 1% of the world's population has autism spectrum disorder, equating to over 75 million individuals worldwide." As it also claims that "Boys are about four times more likely to be diagnosed with Autism than girls" (LevelAhead ABA, 2025). With this, I care to make a difference for these individuals around the world as I'm now in the process of becoming an International autism motivational speaker.

This book, *Everything's Possible With Autism*, is not just a title but a belief as well. So I'm not only hoping to inspire you and your child with my own journey here throughout the book, but to also provide you practical ideas on how to empower your child with Autism to become the best version of him or herself. As much as this book will mostly be about my journey, you will also learn about the Autistic mind and how it all works and also other ideas on what can also be more impactful to break down your

child's Autism barriers as well, as all this will be discussed in most chapters.

This book is not just for the parents, caregivers, or guardians who need the extra

guidance to help better their child with Autism, but it can also be utilized by those with

Autism who need to be inspired and optimistic by my story and also those who need the

perspective on how the Autistic mind is wired differently than most brains. Remember to

keep in mind also that every child with Autism is different, so do not expect to see

amazing results after reading this book, especially on how they can overcome their own

obstacles with Autism. Some may or may not improve with their own Autism after

reading how to overcome obstacles with their own Autism within this book.

So, let's embark on my epic journey together where understanding, acceptance,

patience, timing, and boundless possibilities await when it comes to Autism. Yes, I said

it! It is true that Everything Is Possible With Autism. Enjoy reading!!!!

CHAPTER 1: The Flipped Smile

had a normal and happy life as a baby before things took the wrong turn and then everything turned into a negative. For example, I would even laugh and smile like I would always be enjoying life. Not only did everything taken a downturn later on as a baby, but this was mainly how I learned to become even a better and stronger version of myself with all of the greatest support I've always had.

So my own personal story starts like this. I was born as a normal and happy baby on June 18, 1998 in Torrance, California at the Torrance Memorial Medical Center. After this time, I started to be all smiles as I was always happy and was always nicknamed

"Mr. Smiles."

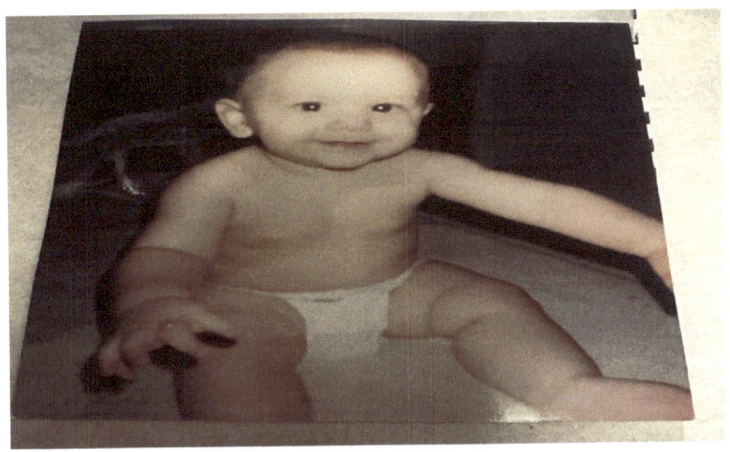

I was always nicknamed "Mr. Smiles."

At six months old, I started to become more alert as my mom would always play

Mozart and Baby Einstein videos on our small TV for me to watch, along with every toy

that would flash on the TV and playing relaxing music, just to help develop my brain. I

would sit in my bouncing chair in our living room and watch it. With this, she would play

every video for me for one hour everyday.

At ten months old, I never crawled but instead stood up and walked. Mostly how I

learned was that my mom put me on a table and let me hold on to the edge of it; and

then I just went and started walking. My mom even put me into Gymboree classes when

I was just a year old just to teach me motor skills and to interact with other babies. I

started to get active as I started to play with toys and started to like Barney and Winnie

the Pooh. Mom also bought me a sit- and- go choo- choo train and I would always play

with it as I loved it.

I started to pick on carpet and then put each piece of it in my mouth and I would start chewing on it. Mom would then take me to the doctor as she was concerned why I was chewing carpet in the first place and second I could have swallowed something. Then she took me to a pediatrician who told and assured her that as long as I was doing daily bowel movements and still eating, it was fine. He asked her also if I swallowed any of the carpet pieces and my mom told him "no" as she would always keep an eye on me every time and would take a big chunk of all of the pieces out of my mouth everytime. Then she would tape the corners of the carpeted floor to avoid me from picking the carpet and stuffing my mouth with it.

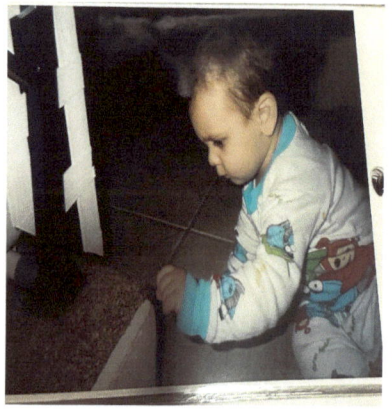 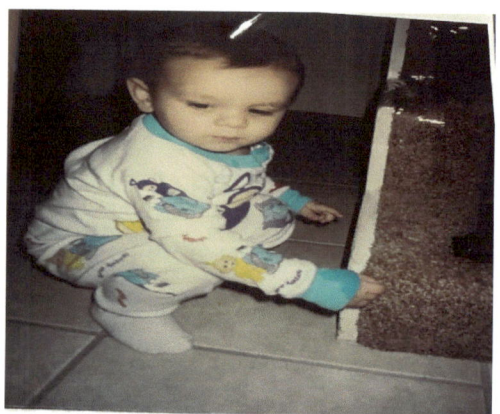

(Left) I always picked at the carpet, piece by piece. (Right) I would pick at the carpet so much that some spots would need to be taped because so many pieces were missing.

When I was just two years old, this was when I started to become more alert and more active. For example, my mom would always take me to Chuck E Cheese when we lived in Redondo Beach, California at this time, and everytime I would see the mouse character, I would always run away from it and would also scream loudly. This was also one of the reasons why my mom never liked taking me to Chuck E Cheese as that place would also get dirty. So, because of this, she never took me there again and instead made our living room at our house a big playroom that would exactly be like Chuck E Cheese, in which it also had play trains, cars, ballpit, slides, and a play tower. So once she did all this for my own entertainment and less fear of any costumed character, I was even happier every time she did this.

Me in a ballpit that my mom built for me.

Both of my parents got divorced during this age in my life as well. So, I stayed with my mom in Redondo Beach as my dad moved to Palm Springs, California.

Also, I received my second set of the MMR (Mumps, Measles, and Rubella) vaccine shot containing both metals of mercury and uranium in it as well; in which I went from having all smiles to all frowns. Of course I would smile some of the times but they wouldn't last very long like they used to. So at this time, I was diagnosed with Autism. It seems like I was no longer "Mr. Smiles" after everything took a slump after the vaccine shot! It was even so difficult for me to speak then as well; a great example of this would be that if I ever wanted something, I would always reach my arm and hand out and say "UH UH!" as both of my parents would always have to guess what I wanted by asking if

I wanted this or that until I would nod my head "Yes." So if I were to shake my head

"No," then of course they would have to keep guessing until I nod my head "Yes."

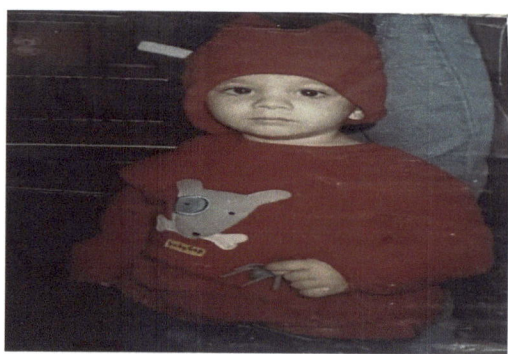

I started to have more frowns after the MMR vaccine shot.

Remember, it does not mean those who are nonverbal and have Autism have no

emotions, don't understand others, or have low intelligence. This is actually the

opposite. Many of those who are nonverbal and have Autism actually possess their own

ways of expressing themselves and understanding others, as they have a high level of

cognitive ability. So sign language and finger-pointing, along with noises like what I did

when I wanted something, is one of the great ways on how they can communicate.

Train your nonverbal child to use sign language and ask them choices like what

my parents did with me. Keep doing this until they are happy with the choice you

provide them. Training them to answer to choice questions by either nodding or shaking

their head would be really beneficial for them to express what they want or need. So do

not give them an item or even do an action until they shake their head "Yes." I will also share later in this book on how I started to become more verbal and how others can do the same as well.

As much as I started to have a flipped smile from the vaccine, everything has began to improve a little bit at a time once I started to be around my dad more. My mom always did her best to spoil me along with help me improve with my own Autism, but she also agreed for my dad to have me more often as he would actually be a better choice to help me enhance even more with my own Autism. Everything keeps improving one step at a time!!

CHAPTER 2: A Whole New Adjustment

s a parent, have you ever thought of making a selfless decision; especially for when it comes to what's best for your child with Autism? Well as much as my mom did everything she could to handle my own Autism for the three years I was living with her, she made the best selfless decision that she knew for me. It would be soo difficult on her own life but would make a greater impact on my own life. I'm always proud to say that if she hadn't made this best altruistic decision, then I would be way different than how I am today. I'm telling you that this chapter will get more interesting, so stay tuned in to this chapter!.

So at age three, I stopped picking carpet, thanks so much to my mom who was always protective of me to where she would keep an eye out for me everytime.

Mom also got me a whole Thomas the Train set as Edward the red train was always my favorite. Plus, another thing of how she spoiled me was that she always took me to a cookie place called Cookies By Design right by our house in Redondo Beach as she would always get me these gourmet cookies on a stick. Those at the cookie place would make them in different characters such as Winnie the Pooh, Mickey Mouse, etc.

(Left) Me playing with my Thomas the Train set. (Right) As much as I've always enjoying eating the cookies from Cookies By Design, I also had a habit of holding them while playing.

Mom also enrolled me in Beach Babies at this time as well. My teacher's name was Ms. Jeny and Mom liked the school because it was privately owned by this lady who believed in the well-being of the children. There were two classrooms filled with five children and two teachers, as each classroom had their own age group.

Plus, another thing of how my mom was protective of me was that she had to baby-proof the whole house that we were living in as she would be paranoid since as I've always been the only child. For example, she set pillows in front of the fireplace so I didn't fall back and hit my head everytime.

The pediatrician who I had at this time referred Mom to a group, as it was a support group for Autistic children. Then, she decided to take me to occupational and speech therapy. She would take me to speech therapy on Mondays, occupational therapy on Wednesdays, and physical therapy once or twice a week to also help with my motor skills. So the symptoms I had for Autism at this time were that I could not speak, I had less smiles and more frowns on my face as I was sad mostly, and I was timid along with being afraid to try new things. With this being said, I was placed in speech therapy to help me speak along with being placed in both occupational and physical therapy to help me try different exercises so I would be less timid of doing them. For example, such exercises would include balancing on a board and climbing.

Mom also enrolled me in the Redondo Beach Unified School District for Preschool and Kindergarten at Alta Vista Elementary School and I was still going to Beach Babies at the same time as well.

So at age four, I started to become more independent as I had my own fire truck and would sit in it and drive it down the street within our own neighborhood. I have always enjoyed riding this fire truck as I really did feel like I was driving a real fire truck everytime I drove it. This was when I really started to become more fascinated with firetrucks as I have always enjoyed watching firefighters drive them and how they use the hose on the back of it; which I also enjoyed the most too. So this fire truck that I had at this time also had a toy hose, which I was of course able to spray water out of it. Now this was why this fire truck was one of my most favorite toys to play with outside.

At age five, both my mom and her boyfriend at the time named Jerry broke up; then she decided to move to Las Vegas, Nevada, to live with her sister (my Aunt Gina). The court stated that she couldn't take me out of state. When my dad was also in court with my mom, he said to her "You're not leaving with my son. So what are you gonna do with him?" She replied, "I don't know." Then he stated "Then you might as well leave him with me." So then, Mom signed the papers to allow my father to have full custody of me. So here was a difficult decision for my mother to make. She decided to make a selfless choice of giving me to my dad as she also thought it would be a better idea for me to go live with my father; he would be much better at dealing with my own Autism than my mom.

Then one day, my father picked me up from Beach Babies, and I started to live with him in Cathedral City, California, from then on. Once my father picked me up that one day, I really had no idea what was going on besides me not talking at all, then, along with everyone including Ms. Jeny, saying bye to me as I was walking out the door with my dad. I even had no idea that I was actually going to live with my dad as I, of course, thought I was going to stay with him for the weekend. That would always happen as he would also pick me up every other weekend to stay with him, my former step mom Rachel, and my former step-brother Justin.

Once moving in with my father, I adapted very well to the change of residency from my mother's house in Redondo Beach to my dad's house in Cathedral City and all the changes in my daily routine. I also had no tantrums and neither was crying, as I was really happy and enjoyed living with my father, Rachel, and Justin. Also before I started to adapt to the change of living with my father, it wasn't even like this while I was living with my mom. While living with my mom, and every time my dad would pick me up every other weekend from Beach Babies, I would always cry every time I saw him when he would pick me up. I always enjoyed being around my mom. So I cried everytime he would pick me up but then would calm down after a while, as I even had no idea that I would stay with him for the weekend. I thought I would really be away from my mom like forever.

But I started to get used to that routine little by little the more my father would spend quality time with me on every other weekend like that. I started to have more fun while staying with them after crying for a while. Then every time my mom would pick me up after my dad dropped me off half-way to meet my mom to get me, I would get excited to see her again.

I also started to attend Landau Elementary School in Cathedral City to finish my kindergarten year. When my family and I made the first couple of trips to school to get me registered, I got upset a little bit and then I cried; I recovered quickly after my father comforted me. I cried and got upset due to the new adjustment of being in a new environment, being around newer students that I had never met, and having a new teacher: this was also something I had to adjust as well. I showed a little anxiety, but nothing remarkable as I was content to go back to school the second day and every day thenceforth. Plus, I would always answer "yes" every time I was asked if I wanted to go back to school.

My motor skills and coordination became better than before. For example, I started to be able to fully undress and dress myself. The only thing I struggled with during this time was tying my shoes; but at least I could sometimes button, zip, and snap my clothes as I was also struggling with these as well. I would also need to be reminded to grasp certain objects in the correct way such as holding a spoon, fork, pen, or crayon as I would often opt to grasp them immaturely and was also discouraged to do so as well.

I was also apt to be inactive and unsociable around other children as I did not initiate play, except for with my former step brother Justin. Everytime during play with him, I would play with Justin in many ways but I was unable to "role play" or perform "imaginative play" with him. For example, if Justin wanted to play fight with his toy animals, I would be at times staring at my toy animals from different angles or even chewing on them. Plus, I enjoyed other types of play such as wrestling around with him or chasing him around the house. The more I played with Justin, I started to get used to it and then I started to enjoy it very much as we started to have more fun together and laugh a lot together. I would even laugh a lot when he did silly things.

Change can really be difficult on everybody, especially for those with Autism. So no matter how big or small a change can be, change can be even harder on those with Autism because their minds are soo used to the same environments, activities, routines, etc. With this, it can take a short amount of time for your child with Autism to cope well with any change; depending how he or she handles it. All you need to do is comfort them and tell them that everything will be ok; just like what my father did with me when I started attending Landau Elementary School and I started to get used to that big change after that. In fact, what could have helped me the most, and it could actually benefit your child too is that my family should have taken me to the school to meet my new principal; and then the principal could then take us on a tour around the school, take us to my new classroom, and to meet my new teacher just any day before the first day of school. So in this way, my mind would already get used to what to expect before going on the first day.

As much as I quickly adjusted to the big change of moving into my father's household from my mother's household, this also made a big impact on my own Autism life along with quickly adapting to the new routines I had to go through while living with my father; they were way different than the routines I had with my mother. Plus, my father got to work real quickly with handling my own Autism on his own that worked out more than how my mother had handled it. Then, I started to change quickly for the better once my father and I really worked together with my own Autism journey. Now this was just for the best!!

CHAPTER 3: The Works Have Begun

Once my father and I started to get to work with bettering myself with my own Autism journey, my stereotypical behaviors would increase every now and then, but at least they decreased overall later on. As my dad started to help me, he also put me on a different routine that was not so fun as it gave me lots of discipline; but at least this was one of the best ideas to decrease my own stereotypical behaviors due to my own Autism. In order to become more successful, especially when it comes to becoming a better version of yourself, sometimes you just need to make the hard and uncomfortable decisions that may not be so enjoyable. But at least life will reward you with what you wish for. A BETTER YOU!!

So after my father would come back home every night from working at Gold's Gym as a personal trainer in Palm Springs, I would go into my bedroom with him and then we would both sit cross-legged on the carpeted floor as I would always sit in between his legs. Then he would teach me how to speak through *Hooked On Phonics* from there, as we would both do this every night. We would always do one chapter per night as he would always teach me how to say one word at a time along with him teaching me how to read out loud to him. The more he did this with me, it always looked like I was going to say each word every time, but it was still difficult at first for me to say them. So my father said each word slowly with me and then it became easier for me to say them. Then the words I said slowly started to build up to where I was able to put sentences together. With this, I became more verbal a little bit at a time.

I also never made eye contact at this time either; in which everytime anyone would look and talk to me, I always had the habit of looking down. So everytime my father would speak to me, he would always constantly tell me, "Austinn, eyes are up here." Then, I would look down again after each time he would tell me this and then he would tell me this again until I stopped avoiding eye contact.

I had also still been eating whatever foods that were fed to me at the time just like when I lived with my mother while I started to live with my father. For example, my dad and Rachel had been giving me snacks that contained gluten and casein as they started to allow me to eat sandwiches on whole wheat bread and lowfat yogurt. As I had been eating these foods, they started to notice a relapse with my behavior in which I became more hyper than usual, louder than usual, and less focused. My other stereotypical behaviors had increased as well such as hand-flapping and screaming. So because of this, the next day on April 7, 2004, Dad and Rachel put me on a strict gluten- free and casein- free diet.

After putting me on this diet, they expected an increase in stims at first as they were hoping to see an inevitable decrease of my hyper behavior after a few weeks. They had also started to put me on supplements a couple of weeks later to help detox the mercury from the MMR vaccine out of the body, in which they first started to give me SuperNuThera (high- potency magnesium, multivitamin, and mineral supplement).

My father Eric, Rachel, Justin, and myself all went to a birthday party for one of Rachel's relatives at her parents' house in Rancho Mirage, California. Once we got there, I was hungry and ready to eat whatever was left out. For example, my father, other people, and myself were out in the backyard as we were sitting at one of the tables. I told Dad that I want to eat, then he replied, "You can't have these," which were the regular tortilla chips that I was allergic too, besides being on the strict gluten- free and casein- free diet. Then after Justin and I got out of the swimming pool after we finished swimming, some lady was giving out some pizza bagel bites on a little plate. I, of course, walked up to the lady for the bagel bites after she asked me if I wanted some, then Dad came up and said, "Sorry, he can't have those."

Then, I started to feel sad inside as much as I wanted to eat one. So while at the party, Dad and Rachel still had to feed me what was allowed on my diet aside from what everyone else would eat that was there. Finally, when it came to singing Happy Birthday, I told Dad "I want cake," which was a big white cake showing with a lot of vanilla frosting. Dad said to me, "No, you can't have cake." Then I started to feel sad even more inside and wished to be a part of everyone else who would be eating cake. So we left after the party to go back home in Cathedral City and then when Dad tucked me into bed that night, he asked me, "Did you have fun?" Then I replied, "Yes." Then he started to say to me "You can't have cake. Sorry," while making a sad face. Then after he said this to me, I started to feel sad as I started to feel isolated from others who were capable of eating whatever they wanted.

Six weeks later from starting my gluten- free and casein- free diet on April 7, 2004, I had also started taking more supplements such as SuperNuThera with 12.5mg P5P (multivitamin supplement) and EnzymAid capsules. I had also started to take 50mg Coenzyme Q10 chewable tablets a week before this began as well. Plus, my father has also purchased some magnesium sulfate (Epsom salt) cream that he used to rub my back with once a week as well.

While on the diet for six weeks, some of my negative behaviors were escalating, along with an increase in screaming and tantrums, but had slowly improved along with a marked improvement in my ability to focus and pay attention longer and an improvement in my speech. I had also expressed myself verbally with the use of longer sentences and showed a greater effort to speak. The general education kindergarten teacher of the class, which I mainstreamed in for forty-five minutes per day had also noticed an improvement in my behavior also.

I was a delightful child who laughed a lot and enjoyed silly play. I also started to enjoy attention along with beginning to be receptive toward affection as much as I had difficulty expressing it on my own. My favorite activities were putting puzzles together and pushing my school bus and firetruck around on the floor at home.

My father also started to make me listen to this motivational speaker and author who has been an alternative medicine advocate named Deepak Chopra every night at bedtime to help me sleep as doing this every night has also helped me to become more of a positive person as well. With this, my father would always play the CD player of Deepak Chopra beside my bed every night and every time I listened, I always listened to the meditation music in the background as Chopra would be speaking. And this was what mostly helped me sleep along with listening to every positive speech from Chopra.

While still on the diet at six years old, my language, speech, and behavior had all improved, even though my diet would likely have had trace amounts of gluten and/or casein because Dad and Rachel continually discovered some of the ingredients in the foods that they thought were free of them. I started to have other improvements as well, such as having the ability to occasionally express thoughts and desires. With this, I started to use sentences that included up to three words. I also began to use pronouns properly as well. In fact, I rarely said my name "Austinn" every time when referring to myself anymore and instead started to say "I." Although I was still in the process of learning to use the pronoun "my." For example, I started to say sentences such as, "I want popsicle," "I need help," etc.

Also with the diet, my stereotypical behaviors of Autism had decreased overall. Examples were that my finger- waving has also lessened as it would usually happen when I would get frustrated; my tendency to look at things peripherally had also decreased, and my repeating of what others said to me had decreased as well.

I also was starting to be able to answer "yes" or "no" to questions as much as I could, though I still needed prompting.

All in all, I had met most of my goals on my IEP as I finished up kindergarten with my teacher, Amy Semmens, at Landau Elementary School.

It is definitely possible to help your child with Autism to become more verbal and to reduce the stereotypical behaviors by doing *Hooked on Phonics* with them and by putting them on a gluten- free and casein- free diet. While teaching your child to speak by teaching them to read, be sure to read each word, one by one, slowly, along with enunciating the sounds of the letters in the words slowly that combine to form every word. With this, be sure your child reads along every word with you slowly while he or she follows your finger on every word.

Besides your child getting all the help from *Hooked On Phonics* to become more verbal, the gluten- free and casein- free diet is really beneficial to help stop your child's stereotypical behaviors as well. Not only will it help reduce the stereotypical behaviors, but it will also help improve his or her bowel movements as well. In fact, I was not only placed on the diet for my own stereotypical behaviors, but I was also placed on it for my own bowel problems as well. At age two, I had a lot of constipation. So because of this, my father mixed MiraLax powder with water for me to drink daily to help reduce my constipation and bowel problems. But the diet really helped me a lot more with my own bowel problems along with my stereotypical behaviors. In fact, while following the diet, my father always had to make sure to keep my foods separate from his and everyone else's.

For example, if he would make waffles in the toaster oven, he would always make sure to put mine in first or else he would have to scrub off the leftovers from his waffles before putting my own in to avoid the cross contamination. So, in this way, the leftovers from his waffles that are not gluten-free and casein- free would not affect my stereotypical behaviors and bowel movements. Following this diet was really difficult for me not only with my father being aware to keep the toaster oven clean before putting my own food in, but also when going out to eat at restaurants as well. So everytime when going out to eat, my father would always tell the server that I was allergic to most things on the menu and that I was following the diet along with him ordering my meal that would be great for my diet. With this, he would always be aware that my meal would contain no gluten or casein.

For example, if he ordered me a burger patty with no bun and no cheese, and then it came back with one of those things, then he would tell the server "no" and to take it back until it came back perfect. So, it may be difficult for your child to follow this diet, but at least there can be some improvements for not only for the bowel movements and the stereotypical behaviors, but also for better cognition as well.

As much as I started to have slight improvement with all my father's help at home, I also started to have some bumps in my Autism journey, especially when it came to not always being perfect with following the strict gluten- free and casein- free diet. I not only had the difficult times due to this, but also one big life lesson I had to understand and get used to as well. But at least the great news about this time was that it was just a quick fix for me to get over after it took a short amount of time for my father to deal with.

CHAPTER 4: The Dislike Of Change

I t took me a bit to realize how much things in life change and that not everything will remain the same every time. Change in routines were really the main thing that would get me upset every time as I would always cry about them. But at least it never took long until my father helped me to adapt to change in different situations; which is also crucial for everyone as this happens a lot in our daily lives.

After I had begun summer school at a new school, as I had done well adjusting to so far, I was also ready to go as I was not upset at first. Once after Rachel and Justin dropped me off at the classroom and then left me, I started to cry a little. I also cried again about forty-five minutes before Rachel picked me up on the second day but I was okay after that.

During my third day at school, I had an unusually difficult day, as this could be from the fact that Dad and Rachel gave me a doubled dose of the CoQ10 than what I would usually take, in which I would always take half the dose of 25 mg twice a day. Instead, Dad tried to give me all 50 mg at once as this could improve focus and energy. So after I took more than usual in this way, my teacher told them that I was speaking out in class inappropriately for the first time. I was clearly upset and was crying when Rachel picked me up from school as this could be due to the fact that she did not come to the classroom like usual to get me. I also did not handle changes in my routine well. I had expectations of what and when things were going to happen and would get upset when that routine was altered. Then once we got home, I started to throw tantrums. I started to cry and scream a lot when everything seemed to upset me. I was fine after Dad and Rachel put me down for a nap after they fed me lunch even though I never slept, but I started to be in a much better mood and state afterward.

At this age, I have always disliked change such as the change in routines. So every time I would cry and get frustrated over them, my father would tell me "Buddy, things change." Then he would talk to me a bit after this topic so I can really understand more about change. After he would tell me this and talk to me, I would start to calm down little by little. Here, I would not only cry to the changes made when my dad or Rachel would come pick me up in the classroom or outside the classroom, but I would cry to changes due to whether something would be done on time or not. For example, I would get used to dinner being ready at a certain time. But if dinner was ready a little later, I would cry to this change as I was always used to the same repetitive routine. So if I would to cry about this situation along with being hungry, Dad would tell me "Austinn don't worry. Dinner will be ready soon. It's just taking a little longer." So Dad telling me stuff like this everytime when I would cry to change got me used to change even more.

Four months later, after following the strict gluten-free and casein-free diet, my mom was not one hundred percent strict in following my diet as I was visiting her for the weekend. With this, there was a negative effect in both my behavior and attention. For example, the first two days of school following the weekend at my mom's were extremely troubled. My behavior was unusually disruptive as I was lacking focus at school. I was then put into "time- out" on the first day and then threatened with time- out on the second day. By the third day of school that week, my behavior had really improved as I was fine by the end of that week. Plus, at least the improvements in my speech, language, and behavior were then starting to become better and better all the time.

I also started to express myself about ninety percent of the time using sentences of approximately three to four words at a time. In fact, I had been making accomplishments every time when I speak just by saying short sentences such as, "No, I don't want to" and "I want …. (such and such)."

So just like what I discussed in Chapter two that change can be difficult on everyone and to those with Autism, besides comforting your child with Autism and telling them that everything will be ok, describing to your child about the change of a situation just like what my own father did can become really beneficial for your child to cope with the change and for his or her mind to easily adapt to it. Be sure after explaining the change to your child to give them time to process what you told them and to also be sure to speak clearly while describing the change. Same goes for when my father explained clearly about the change for when I would cry everytime and then I would cope and adapt more to the change once he would allow me time to process what he told me after that.

Along with coping better at change with different types of routines, I started to progress, little by little, with everything I'd been working on at home with my father to help me become who I am today. So when reading the next chapter, everything was only slight improved but not perfect. Stay tuned!!

CHAPTER 5: Not Perfect, But Slight Improvement

So as much as I was still struggling with some of my stereotypical behaviors, things had started to improve a little bit at a time. So while raising your child whether with Autism or not, just know that it takes a bit at a time for your child to be that great child that you've been wishing for him or her to become. For example, I did not really start to talk a lot right after learning from *Hooked On Phonics*; it took day by day for me to start to improve with my speech a little bit at a time. Then *Hooked On Phonics* became a big help as I started to communicate a lot more, that was when my father thought of another item that may have become more helpful for me than *Hooked On Phonics,* which had a little challenge but not too much as I really had a lot more fun with this one.

Periodically, I would still say my name "Austinn" instead of "I," "me," or "mine" while speaking. Now this was still one of my stereotypical behaviors that I was trying to improve on.

I was still engaging in unusual repetitive play, but many of my other stereotypical behaviors had decreased slightly. My favorite activity then was watching my electric train go around on the train table. With this, my dad helped me make a paper tunnel for the train to go through. At this time, I had always enjoyed trains and tunnels, especially watching trains drive under tunnels, even when I would watch them on TV. So, because of this, I would even drive my train and bus under the tables and /or chairs, pretending that they were going through tunnels. Everytime I played like this, I always wanted to make sure everything including the trains would run perfectly without any problems; as I would get upset if one of my trains would not be working right. The school bus was also another one of my favorite toys as well.

I would also be great at generally answering questions that were being directed at me, but I would still need prompting sometimes.

I started to become better and better at doing *Hooked On Phonics* with my dad every night after Dad taught me how to read one word at a time, one chapter each night. So, because of this, Dad thought, Alright, he's getting great at this. Let's do puzzles! So, at this time, Dad and Rachel bought me a wooden puzzle of the United States, and my father helped me learn all of the fifty states. I then started to be great at the puzzle too as I first started to know about five of the states once after both Dad and I started to do the puzzle every night. From there, Dad would test me on all of the fifty states every night as I then started to become better and better at putting down and remembering each state as each state was a wooden piece. For example, every time Dad would tell me, "Put down Texas," then I would put down the Texas- shaped puzzle piece on the board; same goes on with all the other states. I also became great at remembering a lot of the state capitals too.

So, if your child enhances at an easy activity, such as *Hooked On Phonics*, then start doing a different activity that has a little bit of a challenge that is both entertaining and not so frustrating to do. Same goes for when I started to do the U.S. wooden puzzle after improving on *Hooked On Phonics,* which was a little bit of a difficulty along with the fun, but not so difficult. Plus, even remembering each state by its own shape helped me more at remembering what state it was and where each capital was. Like how the puzzle helped me, doing similar puzzles with your child can also improve his or her memory, social skills, and to develop cognitive skills.

Of course doing the puzzle helped me with both my memory and social skills, but I would say not much in developing my cognitive skills as much as the more I kept doing the puzzle every night with Dad. My memory got improved on where every state goes on the board or map by remembering their own shapes and it helped with my communication by him teaching me how to say every state and capital.

As much as my communication kept improving by both *Hooked On Phonics* and the puzzle, I was still having other challenges that I also needed to advance due to my own Autism. With this, things even became harder for my father as he was told some bad news relating to my schooling because of my own Autism; this was when I started first grade. So things were still bumpy in our paths, but at least he had to make the best decision for me as much as it was not an easy decision for my father to make.

CHAPTER 6: How Autism Really Became Even More Of A Challenge

O nce I started first grade, things have started to become more of a challenge for me due to my own Autism. Plus, things were even more challenging for my father as he had to face some difficult decisions to keep me on track to excelling in the first grade. Of course, I had no idea what was going on at this time while facing all the difficulties I was facing in school. Sometimes in life, we all have to face the most difficult decisions in order to reach success; especially those with Autism.

I was now in the first grade Special Day Class at Sunny Sands Elementary School in Cathedral City, California, and my teacher then was named Ms. Bogie. As I started at this school in September of the year 2004, I had adjusted immediately; there were about eight kids in my class at the time. I then enjoyed school very much as I loved my teacher. I received speech and language therapy twice a week at school for thirty minutes per session and occupational therapy once a week for thirty minutes.

My teacher, Ms. Bogie, was soo awesome that she would even be aware of what the other students and me in the classroom were doing. For example, during the beginning of my first- grade academic year, the other students and myself were doing some classwork that was based on journaling. So, as I was writing in my journal, I started to bite a small pink eraser on the back of my yellow No. 1 pencil. Then, Ms. Bogie came and said, "No! Go sit in time-out." As I sat in timeout in a chair facing the wall, I was crying, and then she started to say, "You cannot eat this; it will go down your throat and hurt your stomach." So as much as I was crying because I was put into time-out, I started to learn and understand more to not bite certain things, especially of what can be harmful.

I started to be afraid of any ball, whether it's a baseball, kickball, football, etc., as I would sometimes get hit in the face by a kickball whether it was during recess or after lunchtime when other children would play together with a kickball. So after getting hit in the face, of course my face would hurt for a quick second and then was gone. Then after this happened, I would cry and then I started to be afraid of the ball ever since. Cause I would be afraid that if I were to get hit again, my face would hurt more than I thought, like more than a quick second.

I also had my three year psych evaluation and Annual IEP meeting. The test results supported the diagnosis of Autism. The recommendation was for me to remain in Special Day Class as my father was asked "Do you want Austinn to be enrolled in Special Day Class or be enrolled in general education class? If he were to be in general education class, then he would not learn as much. If he would to be in special day class, then he'll never be able to graduate with his peers." Then my father replied "We're gonna do what we have to do. So let's do Special Day Class." Plus, I had low levels of comprehension and ability as this was why I was not ready to mainstream into general education class at this time. But the great news was that I had made progress in math and reading and I did not need adaptive physical education because I always did very well in regular P.E.

Here's an official summary of my performance levels then of my psychological and educational evaluation:

Career/vocational: Distractible, short attention span, very cooperative and compliant.

Behavior: Followed class rules, got along well with my peers but required encouragement to interact with them; difficulty staying on task.

Daily Living Skills: Fed and dressed myself, used the bathroom independently. All self-help skills were below average.

Fine/Gross Motor: Visual motor integration was below average. Visual and auditory processing were also far below average.

Social/Emotional: Generally happy and did well with routine; new experiences outside of the classroom can upset me at times; somewhat timid in play situations. Was very timid, dependent, withdrawn and anxious at times. Good natured and well liked. Tended to play near but not with peers.

Description of how my disability affected involvement and progress in general curriculum: Autism prevented my ability to interact effectively and to learn in a typical classroom with grade level curriculum.

I was also able to count to 100 by ones, fives, and tens! I just had trouble adding, but can only do it using a number line.

I had still been on my special GF/CF diet along with taking the supplements of SuperNuThera, Co Q10, and EnZymAid, and I started taking Alpha Ketuglutaric Acid for 5 months and 8 1/2 weeks as well. One day, my father, Rachel, and Justin picked me up from school and Dad said to me, "Hey Austinn! So we went to a store called Clark's today, and we got you special cookies, crackers, etc.!!" After he said this, I was soo excited and soo glad to still be able to eat anything that everyone else eats but in a special diet version. So as long as I was able to eat anything but in a special diet version, I would be happy and no longer sad.

So no matter what type of situation you and your child are in that is making your journey path more difficult, whether this is similar to what my father and myself faced after my father was told that I would never graduate or if it would even be a different situation, just know that there will always be a way to push any type of barrier out of your own path for you to keep going. It is always crucial to never lose hope at what you are trying to achieve in life. In fact, if you want to put your child on the same GF/CF diet as I did, there is even a way to make your child happy and not feel so divided from everyone else when it comes to eating certain foods. My father finding a way to make me happy again by going shopping at Clark's is a great example of this. Every time if my family, or even everyone who I would be around, would eat certain foods that I could not eat, I would still be happy by consuming an alternative of what everyone else would eat no matter if it would to be pizza, ice cream, etc. Along with my dad doing everything he could to push the barrier out of our way to improve more with my Autism in school, life, etc., I started to improve a bit in school. But it was really my stereotypical behaviors that we needed to work on. Plus, my stereotypical behaviors seem to be a bit worse and even weird at this time too.

CHAPTER 7: Improving But Things Are Getting A Bit More Stereotypical

Although I was not doing everything perfectly in school and at home, at least I started to improve a little bit at a time. Along with this, I started to have lots to work on with my stereotypical Autism behaviors as they started to get weirder; this became mostly one of the goals to improve on as well. Other than this, my other behaviors at school and home started to improve as this went with my studying habits.

I still enjoyed trains, fire trucks, and buses. My favorite play was pushing these toys around on the floor and making noises affiliated with them. I also loved to ride my PowerWheels© motorcycle. I was not afraid of going fast and could steer it very well in forward and reverse. I also liked to ride my bicycle (with training wheels) and my Razor scooter.

My stepbrother Justin and I communicated and talked to each other during playtime, though conversations were always generally led by him. My responses were simple and repetitive. Plus, I sometimes resisted or rejected his attempts to play with him.

I was always very obedient and good- natured. I laughed a lot and was happy most of the time. I started to adapt really well to change and did not get affected by it, thanks to my father for talking to me about how things in life change all the time when I would always cry and get upset about change.

Being on the GF/CF diet for ten months now, along with taking four of the supplements daily, I continued to show improvements in all areas, which led both my dad and Rachel to believe that the diet has been working. I still had good and bad days where my stereotype systems would fluctuate either less or worse.

As I received my second trimester progress report in school, my teacher Ms. Bogie indicated that my study habits, though below satisfactory level were improving. This includes my ability to work independently, listen attentively, follow directions, contribute to class discussion and activities and use time wisely. My ability to work neatly and carefully was satisfactory and my ability to complete class work on time was very good. These results indicated my desire to learn and show that I was improving.

I was also performing below grade level in all subject areas (math, reading, language, spelling, science/health, and social studies), which is to be expected in light of my language delays, but I continued to show improvement.

I had also made progress toward all of my IEP goals and was expected to meet at least 2 of the 6 goals set for me. The two goals that appeared that would be met were recognizing a list of 75 sight words and adding and subtracting numbers up to 20 using a number line. The goals that my teacher did not feel would be met were being able to retell a familiar story, blending sounds given to me into words or syllables, identifying time on a clock to the nearest half hour, speak and write in complete sentences when given up to three verbal or visual cues.

Overall, I had shown remarkable improvement over the past ten months. I had really begun to blossom in my speech and ability to communicate and in my imaginative play. I started to play with my stepbrother Justin a lot more than I used to as opposed to playing by myself or "parallel" to Justin. We had begun to interact much more effectively and we appeared to understand each other fairly well.

Sometimes, I understood questions and was able to answer them accurately and sometimes I did not. This went back to the observation that I had good days and bad days.

The stereotypical symptoms and behaviors include:

1. Acting very silly and laughing a lot for no apparent reason.

2. Saying random things that don't make sense.

3. Repeating questions or words (which is generally a sign that I did not understand or did not know how to answer it).

4. My inability to be quiet when asked to.

5. Inappropriate noise level (when talking or singing).

6. Chewing or licking my toys.

I started to infrequently scream or throw tantrums, except for the days of after being disciplined or being put in time-out, I would also throw a small fit (but nothing nearly as dramatic as I used to a year or two before).

My personal goals that I had to work on at home were:

1. Learning how to take a shower and wash my hair and body by myself.

2. Learning how to tie my shoes.

3. Learning how to brush my teeth (correctly) by myself.

My mom decided to move to Las Vegas, Nevada, so it started to become tough for me to see her as often as I used to. So, I only saw her twice a year, especially during breaks from school, like for summer and winter breaks. I would visit her for either a weekend, a week, or even two weeks. As much as I would always get super excited to see her everytime when Dad would drop me off to her, I would always cry on the day of or even a day before Mom would drop me off to my dad for me to go back home after visiting her.

Even with still following the strict GF/CF diet and taking the same supplements, all my other behaviors started to excel as much as my stereotypical behaviors were fluctuating on different days. So here, nothing was always perfect as doing this same routine took a lot of time for me to advance at all the goals we were trying for me to accomplish. I still kept progressing with my academic behavior in the classroom, but I started to develop a bit more stereotypical behaviors, as one of them started to become inappropriate at school and I started to get into trouble with this one. With this though, I at least even started to do even better with my other goals and behaviors at home as well.

CHAPTER 8: Don't Let Anything Stop You!!

Have you experienced any type of stereotypical behavior with your child whether it is weird or inappropriate? Within this chapter, I will continue to share some more of my own stereotypical Autism behaviors that started to become weird and inappropriate, even at school. But at least the great news was that I kept excelling even more with my own goals, especially academically. Along with the stereotypical behaviors, I was still having difficulties with reaching some goals academically, but at least things had started to transcend even more for both at school and home. I was now not letting my own Autism stop me from going beyond!!

So was now seven years old and as much as I'd been following the diet for two years, along with taking the supplements, I had continued to show improvements academically but had some notable behavioral setbacks.

One of these setbacks was that I was displaying odd toileting behavior. At first I started using the bathroom constantly. I would go to the bathroom every ten minutes as much as sometimes I would go to the bathroom, and other times I would try going. This became a problem when I was constantly asking to go to the bathroom, even when I didn't have to go some of the times. I also began putting my hands in my pants often; this also became a problem at school. I even had a few incidents where I would say inappropriate things such as announcing that I was touching myself. I also began to say that my "peepee" hurt. So, Dad and Rachel took me to the doctor for a checkup and urinalysis to see if I had an infection or kidney problem. The doctor and lab tests both revealed that I was fine. My teacher Ms. Bogie, my occupational therapist, and both Dad and Rachel took immediate corrective action to stop the behavior, and eventually after about a month, I stopped putting my hands in my pants. Plus, everytime I put my hands in my pants at school, especially in the classroom, it was even helpful when my teacher told me to stop everytime. In fact, one day, as I was sitting at a big desk with all the other students and my teacher, my teacher caught me putting my hands in my pants.

Then she told me to turn my card to red from it being a green card to start with, as every-one of us had green, yellow, and red cards due to our behaviors in the classroom. Then she told me to put my head down at my own desk after I turned my card to red. I of course was crying after being put into time-out for a bit in this way due to my inappropriate behavior. However, I was also currently continuing to revert back to my toilet-training and bladder control struggles. So, Dad and Rachel had to put me back in Pull-Ups at night-time, as they planned to put me in Pull-Ups during the day if I would to continue to have constant accidents, both at home and at school. This had also become a serious issue that Dad and Rachel were unsure of how to deal with.

One thing they had done was create a "Potty Chart" to reward me for nights when I would not wet my Pull-Ups. After this happened, they were uncertain whether or not it was helping; as to me, it was helping little by little as it also taught me more on how to potty train.

On a good note, my vocabulary continued to increase constantly, and I started to ask a lot of questions. In fact, I sometimes asked questions out of context, as much as Dad and Rachel would know the answer, but at least I attempted to converse. They continued to encourage me to do so. I had come a long way with my speech and language abilities. I had also became eager to communicate as well.

My interaction with Justin had improved as well, as I would sometimes attempt to take the lead in our play-time, especially by "making up" games and initiating play. This was also a huge stride in my social skills as well.

Unfortunately, my biggest hurdle was comprehension, as I had a tough time understanding things. Questions and instructions (unless they are routine learned behaviors) were difficult for me. In fact, I even had a hard time with the question "Why". So, I was able to give solid answers but was unable to give personal descriptive or detailed answers yet. For example, if I were to be asked, "Where is your shirt?" I would answer "bedroom" or "over there" instead of answering with details and in complete sentences. Plus, I was also unable to state what I would be thinking about, explain how I felt, or why I did something. The good note though was that I would at least tell Dad and Rachel if my stomach or head hurt. Unfortunately, I would sometime say something hurts when it would not. So at least I had shown some improvement.

After finishing up my first grade at Sunny Sands Elementary School, I went straight into the Extended School Year program (specifically for students with disabilities) at Katherine Finchy Elementary School in Palm Springs, California. Going to the ESY school every day for 4 weeks was only for 4 hours, but at least it gave me the opportunity to continue learning and staying in the routine of going to school. My teacher was Mr. Manning; I really enjoyed going to summer school.

I still had the same six stereotypical symptoms and behaviors like stated earlier as I started a new behavior, which was sticking my right arm out and twisting it from left to right. Whenever I would do it, Dad and

Rachel would tell me to stop. I stopped doing this behavior after the short time of doing it and being told to stop. Later, I started to scream more often than before, and they were unsure if it was due to something in my diet. So they started to become more aware of following it.

So, I had only seen my mother once for 3 1/2 days since she moved to Las Vegas, Nevada. After seeing her, this started to have a sudden change in my life (emotionally) and its disruption to my routine had contributed to the negative behavior changes that I started to be displaying, besides starting to cry and be upset after coming back home from seeing her. Overall, as much as I had a difficult couple of months after getting emotional from seeing my mother, I managed to continue growing academically and earn awards at school in spite of it. I earned Student of the Month for the first time!!

I could now speak and write in sentences. Although my sentences were not grammatically correct, I was able to communicate fairly well. I was also starting to be able to answer questions more accurately than before. Overall, I started talking a lot as I started to enjoy sharing stories along with loving attention.

I was no longer having any toileting issues. I was completely potty-trained again and did not need to wear Pull-ups at night anymore.

I was also making improvements in all academic areas, though still far below grade level. I was also able to read fairly well as I began a new habit of reading street signs and other signs that I would see while riding in the car with my family. Reading had become one of my stronger areas.

I was doing alright in math but had difficulty in understanding the concepts. I was able to add and subtract using a number line but struggled without it.

I was doing ok socially, as I was no longer shy, but still did not initiate play with other children. I pretty much copied Justin when we would play together and did whatever he would tell me to do, as he was a couple of years younger than me.

My imaginative play skills had definitely improved. But I was not capable of doing role play. For example, if Justin said "I like the blue car," I would say, "I like the red car." Our play would continue in this pattern, with me repeating what he said, but changing one thing about it.

I also started to have a habit of taking out all my toys, especially ones of the same type, and lining them up. Fortunately, I would pick them up and put them away when asked to.

I also started to enjoy building things. I even enjoyed building the things I would see on pictures and attempted to replicate it (as in with Lego's©, K'nex© or Magnetix©). I was very good at this. I was also very good at puzzles, as I was even able to put a spherical puzzle together.

Outside activities I enjoyed were the swings, riding my scooter and driving my Power Wheels© toys. I also liked to climb, as I started to learn how to climb up and over a monkey bar playground toy shaped like an inch-worm once, I went to a park with both Justin and Rachel. It was very high and I was afraid until I finally did it. Now I liked to do it all the time, as it made me really happy. The same goes for a 6 ft high rock wall at the park.

I had also started to improve more in my self-help skills as well. I started to be able to shower and wash by myself, with minor supervision. I also started turning off the water by myself when being finished. Plus, I started to be able to brush my teeth, but not effectively. I still was unable to tie my shoes, as I would usually wear shoes with Velcro© straps. I started to fully dress myself, but did not show awareness of how my clothes were put on. Sometimes my pants would be sideways or the bottom of them were rolled up, and I did not take notice or care.

I had lost a lot of my baby teeth. Dad and Rachel were concerned that I might be pulling them out too soon by playing with them when they got loose. I had a tendency to touch things that were loose or broken (or ripped).

Dad and Rachel had seen a noticeable increase in my own hyperactivity, silliness, and laughter as this went on for a month or two. Plus, I had been waving my fingers a bit more often than normal as the stereotypical behavior of me sticking my right arm out and twisting it from left to right stopped.

Those with Autism learning life skills at a younger age like other children is definitely a possibility, no matter where the child is on the spectrum. Every child with Autism is different, as they have their own ways of learning new things, especially when it comes to life skills. For example, I always learned by someone such as my dad doing a self-care skill with me, as I would learn how to do it; then it would take me some days to process it, and then I would get better at doing it on my own. A great example of this is taking a shower and how my dad taught me every step by watching and telling me what to do as I did it, such as: 1). How to turn on the shower head; 2). How to utilize the shampoo and soap and apply them to my hands; 3). How to wash myself using the shampoo and soap after rubbing them into my hands; 4). How to turn off the shower head.

So, this was one of the ways how I learned a new life skill everytime, or we would even do it together as Dad would tell me what to do at the same time, such as when we would take a shower together sometimes, and he would tell me what to do to wash myself as we go. So, these two ways of teaching your child how to improve his or her life skills, especially when it comes to self-care, can be utilized, or you can use a visual aid, such as pictures of a stick figure or a person doing the steps.

Another helpful tool that can be beneficial for your child to learn the steps of any self-care skill would be a checklist, and after every step is completed, then the child would put a checkmark next to each step. Even though I never used visual aids, doing a life skill together with someone or someone watching me and telling me how to do it was mostly beneficial to me. So if one method of teaching your child to excel at a life skill doesn't work, then try another method that you think may be more beneficial. Performing any teaching method that you think may be beneficial for your child to learn a new skill at a younger age would also make a big impact for when they reach adolescence and adulthood, just like other children that are not on the spectrum.

As much as it took me some days to improve better a little bit at a time with a skill, the duration of your child processing how to do it may vary. For example, it may take many months, years, etc., for your child to know a new skill. A child with Autism starting to learn a new life skill at a young age is just like any other child, to where it will also help them to increase their self-esteem along with building their confidence of living independently once they reach adulthood.

As much as I started to develop some more stereotypical behaviors that turned out to be crazier than the others I'd been having, at least I had actually been improving more on my self-care skills, communication, memory, and my imagination. Everything had started to improve beyond as I started to have newer stereotypical behaviors that made me act silly, though I was always positive.

CHAPTER 9: Improving Beyond!!

n this chapter, you will start to see how far I had started to progress, as much as some of my stereotypical behaviors would still be crazy at times. Whether at school or home, I would perform some types of stereotypical behavior to where they would even drive my dad, Rachel, and my teachers crazy. But other than this, I had started to become a different type of child to where I started to excel more with communicating with others, using my imagination, taking care of myself, playing with other children, etc.

The most noticeable behavioral issue was my extreme hyperactivity at bedtime. It would get worse when my father was present. It even had gotten to the point at times where I was laughing so hard that I did not hear what Dad and Rachel were saying to me, or acknowledge that they were upset with my behavior. Plus, I would even wake up in the middle of the night and then start talking and laughing. I started to do it more when my father scolded me, so they think they might be providing me with positive reinforcement. They had decided to try ignoring the behavior and also offering incentives for good behavior.

They had also attributed my overall behavioral change to an infraction in my GF/CF diet. They did know of several things they'd given me that had gluten in them, which they also started to try to eliminate as well.

As much as I'd been following the GF/CF diet for three years then, as I was eight years old then, Dad and Rachel had not been as rigid with tactile products as they had been. I'd been using any soap to wash my hands, played with Play-doh©, and was in contact with other things that may possibly contain gluten. Despite this, I did not have any negative changes in my behavior.

As I just had finished summer school, I returned to the Special Day Class at Sunny Sands Elementary School for third grade. My new teacher for third grade was Mrs. Horton.

Verbally, I was doing very well. I started to enjoy talking and telling Dad and Rachel about what happened at school. I especially liked to report about other student's "bad" behavior.

My speech had really improved as my sentences started to become longer or more complete. I started to work on beginning questions with "may I" instead of "I want."

I started to have a great memory for numbers, like addresses and phone numbers, but my math skills were weak. I even had a tough time with mathematical concepts. I also struggled with comprehension in general.

I also started to enjoy social settings and playing with other children than I used to, especially those who were familiar to me. I started to enjoy playing with my classmates both in the classroom and out on the playground.

When I recognized someone I knew, I would say hi, and if it were a family member or someone else, I would give them a hug.

One day, the other students in my class, other students from another class, and myself were sitting cross-legged in music class. Our music teacher, Mrs. Reed, started to call on some of us to play some instruments in front of the class, such as trumpets, flutes, etc., so I was so excited once I got called on and started to spin around in circles. So because of my inappropriate behavior of the spinning, Ms. Reed then goes, "I'm sorry Austinn; you do not get to play." I felt so bad once I was told this. Then, the teacher aide of my class named Mrs. J came to me and asked, "Do you want to go back to the classroom?" I replied "No!" Then, she said, "Then you better stop spinning in circles."

I started to use my imagination much more than ever before. I was finally starting to engage in some role-playing as well. For example, I would line up my stuffed animals and then pretend to scold them. This was definitely a step in the right direction, as I started to remember and then repeat what I heard at school. This was also during the times when Justin and I would play "Teacher," as this was definitely one of the amazing role-plays we did while playing together. We would pretend to be the teachers, as our stuffed animals would be our students; we also did this role play most of the time during our play-times. So here, the more I played with Justin, the more it would help me to use my own imagination skills, especially when it came to play time and playing "Teacher."

I was also learning how to swim. I started to be able to swim without floaties on my arms, but not well. I even preferred to swim along the side of the pool where I could hold onto the edge. My fears were jumping into the water from a standing position and going down water slides. Despite my fears, I enjoyed being in the water.

I also went through phases of hyperactivity with peaks in the evening and around bedtime and sometimes during or shortly after a meal.

I had slept well without waking up during the night like I was before, especially with my hyperactivity.

My self-care skills started to improve. I started to wash myself fairly well and dried myself off without help. Dad and Rachel still brushed my teeth for me most of the time, but I brushed my own teeth better than I used to.

I was always happy and content along with enjoying going to school. Plus, Justin and I would get dropped off at school in the mornings and would have about 20-30 minutes to play together on the playground before school started. We always enjoyed this time.

As much as I'd been weak with both my math skills and mathematical concepts, I started to improve more in those areas as both Dad and Rachel asked for some additional help that started to become really beneficial for me to get better at my comprehension as I read. I had also started to improve more in other areas as well such as my imagination, role-playing, and speaking skills as I also started to become more positive and be more in a great mood to where my hyperness would still be out of control. Lastly, I had also started to take such action to where we all know it's bad, but at least it had supposedly been a milestone for an Autistic child as well, including myself.

CHAPTER 10: Now Things Are Really Starting To Mainstream

So, both my father and Rachel had found an amazing resource that would help benefit me in what academic areas I need to improve in. They were also optimistic, as I was also optimistic myself, that the extra support from this resource had definitely helped me a lot in school. Both my speech and reading skills had also started to improve to where they started to get perfect, but I started to develop some of the habits that were at times inappropriate while I was performing those tasks. So, I needed to better those habit while both reading and speaking. Plus, I even started to develop a bad habit to where I even know, too, that it is bad for anyone to do it, but I, at least, was never great at it. Which was even a relief for both my dad and Rachel and even MYSELF!!

Dad and Rachel also hired an outside tutoring agency called Sylvan Learning Center to help me in the areas I was academically challenged in. So I started to attend Sylvan for 1 hour right after school 3 days per week.

According to Sylvan, I started to perform reading at a second-grade level. My actual "ability" to read was somewhere near a fourth-grade level, but my comprehension of what I was reading was very low. Therefore, I started the tutoring program at a high first-grade level and then worked toward a third-grade level. Plus, I was even performing in math at a second to third-grade level. Overall, because of how well I tested in math, I started to only do the reading program at this time.

Dad and Rachel were very optimistic about my own success in the program at Sylvan Learning Center, and they started to do their best to push hard to get me mainstreamed into a second-grade general education class as quickly and effectively as possible.

After having another IEP meeting with my elementary school, I began to mainstream approximately 49% of the time in the areas of math and social science in a second-grade general education class. I was doing okay, but did struggle with some math concepts and appeared to require a little more time than average to complete the work.

I would still get dropped off in the mornings to school with Justin at about 10-20 minutes before school would begin. We both enjoyed getting to school early so we could play on the playground. Mostly, we would always walk to our classrooms together to drop off our backpacks before we would go out and play. After doing this, we would sometimes stick together to play on the playground and other times we wouldn't, as I would either go play with my other classmates or go on the swings by myself.

As much as I attended Sylvan Learning Center 3 days per week for 2 months, Dad and Rachel had to discontinue me going there because of the expense.

My speech has improved drastically. I really started to be able to communicate my own feelings and desires and was especially fond of telling Dad and Rachel what happened at school. I also started to have the tendency to ramble on and go from one subject to the next without stopping to hear what anyone had to say, primarily making it a one-way communication. But I started to make a big achievement by talking and sharing information.

I was still in the habit of reading everything I would set my eyes on as I had not learned the sensible ability to read silently. I also had difficulty with speaking in a low voice and had the tendency to be too loud. I did make a great effort to speak properly and would get upset if I would not pronounce something the correct way after many attempts.

Behavior-wise, I had been very hyper lately as both Dad and Rachel were not sure why, but I would always get hyper because I would always be in a great mood, and I would not know how to calm down and control myself. With this, they were not aware of any changes in my diet or daily activities. I had also been "parroting" a lot more frequently than normal as I started to copy more of what others would say every time.

I'd also been improving a lot more with my imagination and role-playing skills. There would be times when I would "make up" a pretend conversation while playing with Justin.

On a bittersweet note, I had begun to practice the art of lying. This had been allegedly a milestone mark in the life of an Autistic child, so Dad and Rachel were thankful for it. I was never good at it, but I did start to do it. I also started to know that it was wrong as well, which was noticeable by the look on my face while I would lie.

One day, Dad and Rachel took me to the dentist for my first checkup and cleaning. I was a little anxious during the checkup exam and cleaning, and the light was especially bothersome to me. It still is bit bothersome to me when going to the dentist as the brightness from the light still bother my eyes. My X-rays showed that I had at least four cavities. They took me to a specialist to get them filled where I was sedated for the procedure. It was a little scary for me, but I did okay, and the fillings were completed successfully.

Lying is one of the greatest milestones for those on the Autism spectrum, as this is one of the most difficult challenges that they face as well. Most of those with Autism are not really skilled at lying, as it is difficult for them to tell a lie as they cannot even understand a certain lie that they are being told. As much as lying can even help anyone hide away their troubles, at least it is crucially used for socializing well with others. So, if your child with Autism gets better with lying, he or she has reached the milestone, and that is one of them to celebrate.

One of the most common sensory issues for those with Autism is being hypersensitive to fluorescent light, such as being at the dentist. Here, even to this day, I still have difficulty with the bright light at the dentist. So no matter if your child with Autism has a sensory issue with either seeing, hearing, or any of the five senses, the only way to help them get through it is by using certain prompts. For example, I would still wear my sunglasses while dealing with the bright light everytime I go to the dentist as much as that started when I was eight years old. Once my father started to put my sunglasses on me as I started to become afraid of the light, since then, I am okay as the fluorescent light has always been soo bright for my eyes. Using such prompts like hats, sunglasses, headphones, etc. would most likely benefit your child when it comes to certain environments such as with luminous lights, loud noises, etc.

As much as I started to progress more with being more social with other children on the playground at school and with my speaking skills, I have now started to develop more bad habits with my speaking skills, as I started to learn a new skill on the playground that has become another challenge for me to overcome. Nothing was easy while I was facing these bad habits and this challenge, but at least this was one of the ways how my mind got even stronger that has helped me to become my stronger self. You will never become your stronger self unless you take the toughest path to success, not always the straight and easy path.

CHAPTER 11: Autism Is Still Having Me Fall Behind

Throughout my Autism journey so far, I had been going through some struggles with both my communication skills and even when it came to doing the monkey bars on the playground. Plus, when it came to speaking in the classroom, I had always had a bad habit that was difficult to control that got me in quite a bit of trouble. Even with myself getting the support I needed to face one of my challenges, such as on the playground, it was still difficult for myself to get over my fears of overcoming my challenges, such as climbing the monkey bars. With this, my own Autism still made it more challenging for myself to overcome any obstacle that I kept trying to control and face.

One day, Rachel took Justin and me to the Civic Center Park in Palm Desert, California. So, when it came to Justin doing the monkey bars, he wanted me to do them with him, as he was having fun doing them. So, as I was climbing up a tiny ladder to do them, Rachel told me, as I first placed my hands on the first bar of the monkey bars and was trying to reach the next bar over, "Come on, Austinn; you can do it!" Then as she kept saying this, I was still struggling to do it without any help. So, she stated, "Come on, Austinn, you should do it. You're 8 years old, and Justin's 6 years old, so you should do it." After this, I started to get frustrated and cry, as I was trying to reach my hand out to do it but couldn't because I was always afraid I would fall and bleed. I was always afraid of blood, as no one was helping me at all to climb to the other end of the monkey bars.

In fourth grade with my different Special Day Class teacher, Mrs. Rieber, I would always go to another classroom for general education math after lunch. One day, I was talking to myself and humming as I have always done as the third-grade general education teacher named Ms. Lehmann was teaching the class. After I got done with this class, she then walked me back over to my classroom to tell my teacher's aide, Ms. Donna, what I was doing as she was telling her that I got detention during recess the next day.

When it came to me doing this type of behavior in my class, I would sometimes get into big trouble, such as detention, and then I would feel so sad and disappointed every time this would happen. I even started to feel really bad once Ms. Donna was told that I got detention the next day. So when detention came the next day during recess, I wasn't feeling much sadness, but at least it has taught me what behaviors were appropriate and inappropriate in the classroom.

Along with facing such challenges and obstacles in the classroom, playground, and everywhere I was at, I started to have someone special come into my life who both my father and myself just met right after my father's divorce with Rachel; as they both got divorced due to them arguing daily. Once this person started to come into my life at this time at eight years old, my life started to really change for the better, as it has gotten easier to overcome my own bad habits along with the obstacles due to my own Autism.

CHAPTER 12: Someone Special Has Come Into My Life

Once I started to have someone special come into my life who had always believed in me as she helped my father raise me, she also helped me beat the odds of whatever obstacles I was having difficulty facing. With this, she helped me achieve things at whatever I desire, regardless if there had been others who never believed in me and would state that I would never achieve these things. So, with all of her support, my own Autism was no longer holding me back from doing all the things that I had been wishing to accomplish.

Dad and Rachel happened to get divorced, so both Rachel and Justin started to move to Orange County, California, so it was only Dad and myself in the household. Then shortly after, we both met someone by the name of Jessica at a restaurant called YardHouse, as both Dad and I would go there mostly throughout the week for dinner after he would pick me up from the after-school program at my elementary school. So every time we would go, Jessica would mostly be our server. After meeting her this way, both my dad and her started to be together, and she started to become a special stepmom figure to me.

Jessica was told by those being in charge of me, especially when it came to one of my IEP meetings at school, that I would never graduate with my peers, would always stay in Special Day Classes, and would never be successful at life. Jessica then said, "No, that is not gonna happen. He just needs someone to believe in him." So she started to help me a lot from there with school, life, etc.

One day at ten years old, as Jessica and I were leaving home to take me to school, and as we both got into her car for her to drive me to school, I was still having a difficult time tying my own shoes as she looked at me in the back seat struggling. As this happened, she told me, as I was close to graduating elementary school, that, "If you don't know how to tie your shoes, especially when you get to middle school, then kids will start to make fun of you."

So then, she started teaching me how to tie my shoes in the simplest way possible, as she then moved to the back seat with me and then started to untie her own shoe and then starts showing me in the easiest step-by-step way on how to properly tie my own shoes. From there, those easiest steps started to stick in my mind and then I no longer struggled tying my own shoes at any time.

As much as Jessica had started to become an amazing role model for me, she had also made me go through some challenges for both my other obstacles and even some of my fears. Even in the next chapter, I will share more of my struggles and some of my fears that I had to face, but at least I will explain in the upcoming chapters how both my father and Jessica have done more to help me overcome them. I will at least explain a bit how they did so in this next chapter with one of my fears and struggles. In fact, when I explain a bit in the next chapter on how they did so with one of my challenges that I had to face in school, I will share how they have taught me a very valuable piece of advice that I have started to keep in mind as I started middle school.

As much as I started to become more able to overcome any of my obstacles, a little bit at a time, as Jessica had started to help me all along every time, my Autism journey had started to become more difficult once I started fifth grade and then middle school.

CHAPTER 13: Sense What?

So during the start of my fifth grade year and onto middle school, I had to face some struggles of my Autism journey. The struggles I had to face were the obstacles and fears that I'm sure everyone else can face in life, and not just those with Autism. For me, not only was this the case for the fears, but I also had some sensory issues associated with those fears that had become the big struggle that I needed to improve upon. Facing both the fears and obstacles at school and outside of school, both my father and

Jessica supported me a lot to overcome them, so they can no longer stay as my weaknesses.

I started playing baseball with the other kids on the baseball team of the Oakland A's and got hit by the ball a couple of times (first at one of our practices as the ball slipped out of my glove to hit my nose after one of my teammates threw the ball for me to catch it and the second time when another kid on another team at one of our games threw the ball accidentally at my helmet as I was ready to hit the ball), so I started to be more afraid of the ball. So with this, I started to become more nervous during the games and started to be afraid if I would accidentally be hit again on the head when in batter's position.

One time, I was trying to hit balls in the batting cages before a game, and I couldn't even hit most of them, as all those baseballs being thrown at me were soo fast that I was even more afraid that they would even hit me in the face. So that's what made me miss all of them as my mind was always obsessed with how painful it would be if I were hit in the face again, even though it only hurts for a few seconds.

I had always been afraid of spiders, as I always think about how bad they can bite, regardless of their size. So Jessica started to make me do immersion therapy just by making me touch the small spider that she found in our backyard and that she froze and put in our freezer inside our house. So for a bit during my breakfast time before school, she would then take out the frozen small spider in a small glass bowl that she caught and froze and then ask me, " You wanna touch the spider?"

I would then hesitate and get scared, especially while she was showing it to me and started to move closer for me to touch it. Then she said, "Touch it!" Then I slowly reached my hand out to touch it as I started to get more nervous. She then said, "It's dead!" Then after she would say this, I would finally touch it. As to whether a spider would be alive or dead, I would always think about how much it could bite and how creepy it looked. I'm still a bit afraid of spiders, but not as much during the time before when she made me touch the spider, as it seemed like it had made me stronger a bit to not have to be afraid of spiders.

I also finally graduated from Sunny Sands Elementary School, and I was soo far proving to those being in charge of me wrong and that with my own Autism, I could accomplish anything, as I had been staying more on track academically.

At age 11, I started 6th grade at James Workman Middle School and was still mostly in special education classes. In fact, I would even take a special education math class, as I would also take the same language arts class for two periods along with taking P.E. and regular classes for both science and social studies. With this, I couldn't even take a fun elective class that I've been wishing to take, but at least I understood that all 3 classes within 3-4 academic areas were the main priority other than the fun stuff in school.

Well, P.E. was always the only fun class for me then anyway! As much as it was the only fun class for me at this time, I also struggled somehow to get an A in it. It was even difficult somehow for me to run faster, for me to pass the mile, and for me to do a lot of push-ups. In fact, I couldn't even go all the way down to do a proper push-up. So, it made sense to me once I got my report card for the trimester of all the grades from all my classes that I got a C in P.E. So then, both Dad and Jessica went, "There's no way you're getting a C in P.E.!" as I told them about the mile and the push-ups after they questioned why a C in P.E. (as it should be an easy A).

So at this time, they both started to make me run more on the treadmill, like walk for 5 minutes to warm up and then run for 10 minutes on the treadmill before walking again for 5 minutes to cool down. And they of course taught me how to do a proper push-up, along with working on no longer sticking my butt up when doing them. All in all, they also told me, "School is your job and training at the gym is our job." So, them saying this to me has also made me keep in mind that getting great grades and an A in P.E. class on my next report card was also my job and to make those who were my support system proud.

During sixth grade, I started to get picked on a lot as it was only verbally and not physically. During P.E. class one time in the locker room before class started, I got messed with by the other boys by showing me their bruises in my face as they were fake sneezing in my face, so I screamed as they were doing it. Then, my soon-to-be seventh grade P.E. teacher named Mr. Hershberger started to go, "Hey! Who's screaming like a little girl in here?" Then the other boys said it was me. So, the P.E. teacher said, "Uh uh! Don't scream." As I was told that, I felt ashamed and embarrassed of myself after screaming and being scared after being messed with. Not only would other students do those two things to me at any time at school, but they would tell me jokes such as "Ooh Austinn. I'm telling on you," even though I never did anything wrong. Then, that would of course cause me to have more anxiety everytime by those jokes because I took things that literally. The main reason why I started to get picked on a lot at this time during middle school was because I took things literally.

As much as this chapter is mostly about my sensory issues due to my fears, with both my father and Jessica telling me that my job was school as the gym was theirs really benefited myself to keeping in mind how I could excel academically. At the same time, I still struggled to study to do well in school as they both were still guiding me to overcome my fears, along with some more of the obstacles I had to face. Not only did they help me academically and with my sensory issues over my fears, but they also helped me to control my stimming and one of the inappropriate social behaviors I was struggling to control as well. With this, I was even struggling to build friendships as I never knew the concept of the importance of building connections, so I never had any emotions with this struggle even.

CHAPTER 14: The Overcoming Of My Stimming, Social, and Sensory Issues

The beginning of my middle school days was the time when I started to face the most amount of challenges; as of course it was due to my own Autism. But the great news is that at least I had both my father and Jessica assist me to become stronger by overcoming them. The challenges I had to face were academically, stimming, and my own sensory issues leading me to my fears. Not only this, but what made my middle school days harder was myself struggling to socially interact with others, which led me to be alone always at school. Even at lunchtime! But my social issues took a bit more time for me to overcome though.

One day during lunchtime, Jessica brought me lunch from In-N-Out as she gave me a double, double protein style burger with two burger patties with lettuce and tomato wrapped in lettuce with fries. So, as I walked her to a table in the multipurpose room, she said to me, "You sit by yourself? That's terrible!" I did not feel any emotions once she told me this, but I also had nothing to say when she told me later on at night at home in Palm Desert, California about how it was terrible of how I sit and eat lunch by myself, along with telling me "Sorry." I felt fine after she talked to me about this because I never knew how to talk to people and make friends as I never knew what having a friend was like.

I also had bad grades in my classes as I never knew how to study, as this was also why I would fail tests too. When it came close to every exam, I thought it was magic to where I would still be ready for every exam even if I wouldn't study much for it. So because I never knew any great studying habits, I would sometimes skim quickly through a textbook, depending on what exam it was or I just wouldn't study at all.

I started to become less afraid of riding my bike with two wheels once Jessica talked me into being brave and not fearing certain things, such as riding my bike. Every time when I would see a bike with two wheels without an extra wheel or two, then I would be afraid to ride it as I had been imagining falling off on my head while riding and then blood spilling out of my head after falling as my head would crack open. So, once Jessica told me that, then every time I would be afraid to do something, I would need to tell myself "I'm gonna do it. I better not be a chicken!" She also taught me how to easily get on my bike before riding it as I was telling myself this then I no longer was afraid.

Jessica taught me the easiest way to get on my bike by telling me a great idea to first put whatever foot on a pedal while still standing up, then you push the pedal with that foot, put the opposite foot on the other pedal, and then you start to sit down as you go. I definitely found this idea to be much easier and beneficial rather than sitting down first before pushing the pedals.

Another thing she taught me to do that made me less afraid was that our bodies make coagulants and make more blood as I was also afraid of falling off my bike and having my head crack open and then blood spilling everywhere. So now I know that if this were to ever happen, our bodies would always make more blood for us to survive as our bodies will make the coagulants, such as platelets, to help stop the bleeding.

Dad helped me stop my stimming (making faces in the mirror, spinning around in circles, and making awkward hand movements, such as sticking my arm out and moving my hand in a circular motion) as one time at home, he told me right in front of my room, "Austinn, you can't be doing that in public. People will think you're weird. If you're gonna do that, you need to do it in your room with your door closed. You have the mirrors on your closet doors in your room if you ever wanna make faces in the mirror and spin around in circles." So, within a month later, I had stopped my stimming as, of course, I would do my stimming in front of my closet doors in my room every now and then, but I even have stopped doing them in front of a mirror later on too.

At twelve years old, I would even laugh for no reason as Jessica would always ask me, "What's soo funny to you right now?" Then I would mostly not know how to answer it or even answer it sometimes, depending on if I would be comfortable at sharing a funny thought or what I would have in mind. Then sometimes, she would get mad if I did not know how to answer it, as Jessica was actually teaching me that we only laugh if something funny happened or if someone would be telling a joke. But I would always laugh when nothing funny happened most of the time. Overall, her getting mad at me actually taught me that we can only laugh at the appropriate times, such as someone telling us a joke, watching something funny on TV, etc. and not when nothing funny is happening.

So, when it comes to the Autistic mind, stimming is definitely caused by sensory issues in most cases. Well not for me, especially when I was younger. Remember, everyone on the spectrum is different, so they all have their own reasons for why they stim besides the sensory issues. For example, I stimmed a lot because I would get excited or happy, as that was how I got all of my positive feelings out. With this, those with Autism may stim due to the same reason as mine or it may be the negative feelings that they have too such as anger and frustration. Even a loud and crowded environment may cause the stimming as well as the more they feel anxious or nervous, the more likely the stimming can happen. So there are various reasons besides these ones that can cause someone with Autism to stim as even boredom is another reason too.

When it comes to sensory issues, someone with Autism may be sensitive to any of the five senses such as: 1). Sights; 2). Sounds; 3). Smells; 4). Tastes; 5). Touch. So those with Autism respond in two ways to any of these sensory issues which are both: hypersensitivity (which also results in sensory avoidance, such as covering ears while being in a loud environment, avoiding certain foods, clothing, etc.) and hyposensitivity (common one in which those respond by making a movement such as making loud noises like screaming, rocking their bodies back and forth, etc.). Plus, someone on the spectrum may likely feel overwhelmed to where they would get a sensory overload. When this happens, it can lead to someone feeling anxious as well as wanting to escape the environment they're in and even make it harder for them to communicate. So, with this, it makes it difficult for someone on the spectrum to cope with one of the sensory issues as their brain can shut down one or more of the functions, such as running away from the environment and being unable to communicate because of the more anxiety that person has.

So, there are various ways for how you can help your child with Autism overcome the stimming and the sensory issues, as certain accommodations would be beneficial, depending where on the spectrum your child is on. For example, it was really helpful of what my father and Jessica told me, like what I shared in this chapter, that helped me overcome my own stimming and my sensory issue of not being afraid of seeing a two-wheeled bike and riding it. Besides this, if you think that your child can process the information easily by you telling them the same thing of doing all the stimming in their bedroom to get all the emotions out, along with telling them why they shouldn't be afraid to perform a certain task due to the same sight sensory issue I had, do it. Otherwise, find something else that would help them feel more comfortable with their own sensory issues, such as: giving them more comfortable clothing; giving them certain foods that they would be more satisfied with due to the textures, temperatures, or spices; wearing sunglasses to avoid bright lighting; wearing headphones in loud settings; and even try putting on two small training wheels on the back of their bike if they also have the anxiety of riding a two wheeled bike like I did.

And for the stimming, also find something that would help them overcome their own stims if they only seem harmful to them and/or distracting to others (examples are: head-banging, ear-clapping, hitting oneself, nail- biting, etc.) such as: giving them a fidget spinner, placing them in a quieter environment where they will be more satisfied and where they can cope as the environment can include no bright lights and soundproof windows, and even by giving them soundproof headphones. Or else, it is ok as it helps them get their emotions out. I would even say that if the non-harmful and non-distracting stimming becomes too much to others publicly, then find a quieter place to where your child with Autism can release all the stimming, along with the emotions out; just like what my father told me to do once earlier in this chapter where I would do the same in my room, whether after we would come home from being out or even when having company over at our house. So, in this way, there would be nobody watching!! Overall, find something that you think may benefit your child with Autism besides all the examples I just provided for you.

Besides overcoming my own stimming and sensory issues, in which again the sensory issues led to me having my fears, I even started to do better socially and academically during the next year of my seventh grade year of middle school. Plus, I even started to become the better version of myself of what I have been dreaming of becoming!! Dreams become true, no matter if you are on the Autism spectrum or not. Always include those with Autism as they are, of course, like everyone else; they just have a special ability!!

CHAPTER 15: Proving Them Wrong

My seventh grade year of middle school was definitely the year when I started to become my dream self. As I started to improve more in school and to control myself from laughing for no reason, I also learned more from my father and Jessica on how to fit in with the other students at school like what most students do, which is how to build a social life and make friends. As much as I still never knew how to form and start a conversation with others, I was starting to grasp the importance of what my middle school years should be like besides focusing on my studies. So enjoy reading the next part of my Autism journey here on how much my life with Autism started to adjust for the better!!

I was still getting bad grades at the beginning of the school year of my seventh grade academic year until one day, Dad told me, "Study until you're ready for it." I was about to sit at the dinner table in our kitchen to study for my first exam for seventh grade for my World History class after asking him, as he was sitting right in front of me, on how to study. I don't think I did great on this test, but at least I had the idea of how to study, in which that tip has helped me to start passing the other tests that I had during that school year and then my grades for all of my classes started to improve because of it.

At the end of my seventh grade academic year, Dad and Jessica taught me how to make connections and make friends especially by asking, "Hey, can I sit and eat lunch with you guys?" Once they both picked me up from school one day and then they asked me, "How was school today?" and "Did you eat lunch with anybody?" and me replying back with "Good" and "No." They also asked me, "Do you like sitting by yourself?" Then after I replied with "Yeah," they asked me, "Why do you like sitting by yourself?" Then I didn't know how to answer that, and then Dad said "It's boring." After this, Jessica told me how everyone would hang out with others and sit with others and how they would even hangout with a big group of friends. So after she said all this to me, I started to get the idea on how people make connections and how it's actually really important to do so as well.

So, the next day at school during lunch time, I asked a couple of boys who I knew named Austin and Nick, as I walked up to their table, "Hey! Can I sit with you guys?" Then they went "Sure!" So after I joined them, I actually started to enjoy hanging out with others more than before, as I started to know the importance of having a social life and make connections. So from that day until the end of the school year, I started to hang with those boys who I knew during every lunch period.

Along with learning "R" sounds in speech therapy, as this was why I had always taken speech therapy since first grade as I have always had trouble saying words that begin with an "R," I also started to learn how to create conversations as well. Dad and Jessica asked my speech therapist to teach me how to make conversations with others, as this had started to help me as well.

When it came to my IEP meeting at the end of 7th grade, my former 6th and 7th grade special education math teacher named Mrs. Eiser, who was also my case worker and was in charge of my IEP meetings at the time, said to my dad and Jessica that "Austinn now has straight As in all of his classes." So, I was super proud inside and couldn't believe that I got good grades, such as straight As in all of my classes for the first. So when me, Dad, and Jessica left my middle school, Dad said to me, "So you got straight As huh? Nice job!" I was even super proud once he told me this as well, as I couldn't believe that I started to study more and push myself to do better, besides them both telling me before that school was my job and training people was their job. With this, I have actually reached my dream of becoming a straight- A student that I've been imagining of becoming!!

Once I transferred to a different middle school for 8th grade called Palm Desert Charter Middle School in Palm Desert, California, when I just turned 13 years old, it was such an exciting day that my father took me to the middle school just so I could pick out whatever electives I wanted to take with my other classes. I never got the chance to take any elective classes during 6th and 7th grade because of being enrolled in all special education classes, such as taking special education language arts class during two periods back to back then too. So, the elective I chose to take for my 8th grade academic year was Robotics, as I found this class really interesting as you would build any type of robot out of Legos©, and then you would program them through computer technology so you can control and move them.

So for this academic year of eighth grade, I had started to mainstream into all regular classes and no longer needed special education classes with all As, along with being awarded twice with a 4.0 GPA honor roll all throughout the year. With this, I had definitely started to become prouder, along with seeing myself more as a straight- A student and no longer a failing student. I started to know more studying habits of what both Dad and Jessica taught me.

When I was fourteen years old, I got awarded the Student of the Month, along with getting all As, during my freshman year at Palm Desert High School. With this, I remember getting the proud moment when a few girls with ASB (Associated Student Body) came into my English 1 class and them pulling me outside of the classroom to award me with the Student of the Month certificate. This had definitely made my whole day greater than I could have ever imagined, as I started to get more of the prouder moments of how much of a longer way I had come from being in elementary school and middle school in all special ed classes and not doing so well with failing grades and no studying techniques and how I was unable to focus in my classes then too. At least I now had started to become the better version of myself with better grades and studying techniques along with now having focus and concentration in my classes.

I stopped laughing for no reason as I started to mature and realize more that we only laugh when someone tells a joke or if something funny happens once Jessica started to teach me more of the appropriate times when to laugh every time when I would laugh out of the blue. With this, I even started to feel prouder with how much I had matured and started to know the appropriate times when to giggle. This was, especially with knowing more of what she taught me that has made me feel comfortable with not looking awkward publicly and me no longer laughing for no reason while being around other people.

Mostly those with Autism would have trouble fitting in with others and building a social life to where they would make friends due to several reasons. Some of these reasons are: **1. Social Cue Difficulty:** Here, those with Autism have difficulty with understanding nonverbal cues such as body language, facial expressions, and the tone of voice that someone else is using. As these social cues can be hard for someone with Autism to understand, this is what is crucial for building friendships. If anyone can't understand the cues, then how will someone interpret others' emotions and intentions? **2. Communication Troubles:** This one was also why I had difficulty with building a social life and making friends, especially in middle school. As like myself, those with Autism would mostly have difficulty with starting and enduring a conversation. **3. Anxiety:** This reason happens due to past difficulties or misunderstandings in social situations that those with Autism were in. So, because of this, someone with Autism would most likely worry about being rejected or making a mistake within a new social setting. Overall, this would cause them to avoid becoming a part of any new social setting.

Remember, just because most of those with Autism are having difficulties with building friendships does not mean they are never interested in doing so. They of course want to build friendships like everyone else; it is just the fact that they need the extra support on how to become more involved within a social setting. So to help your child on the spectrum to become more involved in a social setting, if your child is able to communicate with others without a problem, then go ahead and teach your child to ask another student or even a group of people if he or she can sit with that person or group such as during lunchtime at school, just like what my father and Jessica taught me to do. If you don't think that this same idea would help your child to become socially better publicly, then I have seven ideas that may help your child with that as well as how to better reduce anxiety before entering a new social setting. Here they are: **1. Role-Playing:** This tool can be a great start for someone on the spectrum as I even did this one for a bit while in speech therapy in middle school as well. Role-playing can help your child to learn how to inaugurate a conversation one on one, as well as of course identify the social cues like I discussed in this chapter and learning how to take turns while communicating. **2. Social Stories:** This is used to explain disparate social situations and to teach your child how to handle friendships. **3. Nonverbal Communication:** Teach your child how to observe various social cues such as eye contact, facial expressions, body language, and tone of voice. **4. Small Group Playdates:** Having your child start with one-on-one or small group playdates will help benefit in decreasing his or her stress to where it will be less challenging for your child to interact with others. **5. Teach Coping Skills:** This is a great tool to help your child to manage emotions, such as frustration or anxiety, as these two emotions can make it harder for your child to become a part of a social setting. So, to help with this, teach your child some breathing exercises, give them some sensory toys, or even put them in quiet spaces, as quiet spaces can help your child to adjust his or her emotions for when they feel overwhelmed. **6. Teach How To Identify Emotions:** Teach your child how to recognize their own and someone else's emotions; such as teaching him or her when someone is happy, sad, bored, or even frustrated. Doing this can help improve socially with others. **7. Patience and slow it down:** Patience is key!! It may even take time to find a new friend. Have your child to understand patience and to never give up and try again if an interaction has failed with someone that your child wishes to become friends with.

At least I started to get the concept of the importance of building friendships and having a social life once my father and Jessica taught me how to ask others at school if I can join them. While I would hangout by myself, such as at lunchtime at school, it never bothered me as I still felt happy. I never understood the concept of friendships in the past, along with not knowing how to start a conversation with others. And again like in Chapter fourteen, I never had any emotions also, so I never knew how to feel about being alone and having no friends, as I never knew how to make friends then as well. So along with doing well both socially and academically with my own Autism, and let's not forget about no longer having the laughter for some reason, I have started to really dive into doing bigger and better things than I have even been imagining doing like everyone else does. I have also started to achieve some of these bigger things, as I have also started to become a much better high school student than I have imagined with a bigger reward. This next chapter will amaze you even more!!

CHAPTER 16: Started To Dive Into The Bigger And Better Things

n this chapter, you will be surprised as I will share with you some of the things that started to enhance on, as most of these things are based outside of high school. Although I did receive a greater reward in high school, as I still have improved all my grades to be where I want them. Thanks to my better studying habits!! Autism has no longer been my barrier from myself reaching my own desires in life. So, this chapter will give you or your child on the spectrum a bright idea with how the odds with Autism can be beaten; as you will continue to follow along with my Autism journey and how everything within my own Autism life has started to be more on the positive side. As you continue to read along, tell yourself "Everything Is Possible With Autism and nothing can stop me."

During my sophomore year at Palm Desert High School, I started to study the manual on becoming a personal trainer for when I would turn eighteen. So with this, my father one day asked me, "Are you sure you wanna be a trainer?" Then I replied, "Yeah." Then he replied, "Alright, you got four years to read this manual," as he then started to give me the personal trainer's manual. So, during those four years of high school, I would even start reading the manual mostly on the days when I would not have soo much homework and studying for other tests for my other classes.

When I turned fifteen, my father bought me a small Chevy Silverado 2002 truck especially for me to start practicing driving for when I would get my driver's permit. He also bought this truck from one of his friends named Scott, as he'd been having this truck for a while as I also got involved into buying this truck with my own savings.

Myself when I was fifteen years old and my white Chevy Silverado 2002 truck that I started to practice driving in.

Dad started to teach me how to drive on a private street close to our house in Palm Desert, as he would let me drive his own big, lifted black truck that he had at that time too; he would even teach me how to park correctly in a parking lot by that private street as well. At times, we would even take my new truck out to practice driving on that same street as well.

My father Eric's big, lifted black truck that he would let me practice driving in. Yes, that is also our two seadoos as well.

Before starting my sophomore year of high school, I also started to take karate once my mother started to enroll me in it as well. Once I started my first day of karate during the summer time before school started, I started to enjoy learning the easy self defense moves that I could easily remember, as I even felt proud learning how to easily break a piece of wood in half by folding my thumb and fingers in while holding my hand up, then I would punch that hand to break it. From there, I started to feel proud every time when I would learn a new self- defense move, even though there was never a need for me to defend myself as I had never even been in a fight. It's still always amazing to learn a new move as you never know when you'll need to use it.

Plus, I even enjoyed karate every time I go to where my Kiai would be louder than everyone else's in the dojo. Everytime when I would strike a kick or a punch for example, each Kiai would sound more like a scream to where I would always yell "EE-YAAAAAAH!!!!!!"; as I would always imagine myself escaping a situation to where two or more enemies would try to kidnap me, and I would show off my crazy and loud Kiais and every amazing self-defense skill I have learned to scare them away and even hurt them. At the beginning when I started karate, I was even shy at first to make a Kiai at every striking move, but later on, as I started to feel more comfortable learning every move all along, I then started to have more fun and go crazy with my loud Kiais, as I felt that my own self-confidence has boosted.

At age sixteen, I started studying Driver's Ed once my father gave me a website to the DMV to start studying the Driver's Ed manual; even before my junior year of high school started. So, I would at times still practice driving with my dad while studying the manual all throughout my junior year.

At the beginning of my junior year, I reached blue belt in karate, then stopped after that to focus more on school, as my father discussed with me along with asking if it would to be best to stop so I can focus on my studies. So, with this, I agreed as I could still focus more on getting great grades to graduate.

On the day I turned seventeen, I started to become a member of the NSHSS (National Society of High School Scholars) once I got a letter and a T-shirt with a front logo saying NSHSS from them in the mail. So once I got all these goodies in the mail, I started to feel more accomplished and proud that I have never received such an amazing academic award like this, especially on my special day. Besides getting all A's and the 4.0 GPA honor rolls I had always gotten, I even felt more gifted once I received this award of being a part of something that I never even heard of before.

I got my driver's permit after passing the written test on the computer at the DMV a month after I turned seventeen, as I started to practice driving more with my dad in my truck along with him enrolling me in Miller's Driving Academy to help prepare me for my driver's license. I have always enjoyed and felt more comfortable driving after a driving instructor for Miller's would pick me up, and I would be taught how to drive on a public street and on the freeway (as each session was two hours as the first session was learning on the public street and the other session was learning on the freeway). So, I would feel more comfortable after every time they would teach me how to drive, as I would even have lots of fun driving on the freeway as I would feel like a race-car driver every time I would need to pick up my speed on the gas pedal at 60-70 mph from driving at 45 mph on the street.

Me starting my first driving session with Miller's Driving Academy

So as much as I started to learn more skills based on what everyone else does, such as learning how to drive, taking karate lessons, and even studying how to become a personal trainer while going to school, I had also started to realize even more that no matter what someone on the spectrum does, whether it's big or small, it can become achieved regardless. Even same goes with someone with Autism achieving amazing things academically like myself of how I got rewarded to become an NSHSS member just because I now had been having the better studying habits to get all As in my classes. Here with this great academic award, I felt that I had become a great role model not just for those with Autism, but for everyone that you can change struggles into success.

Just like earlier in this book how I struggled in all my classes in middle school and having bad studying habits, now look how much I no longer struggle in all my classes because of the great transformation with my own studying habits. Besides everything on my Autism journey going from negative to positive, I had started to become grateful of the person I had become. Due to my own Autism superpowers and how I feel that I have set a great example for those with Autism, Autism is never a disability and it's a possibility that even those with Autism can create their lives how they want them to be, and there's no way that Autism can block their paths for that. So the final chapter will be the rest of my Autism journey as what you will read in the next chapter will share with you why I am really grateful of who I am today. So all the things that I even have been trying to improve upon have become the greatest achievements as you will read what they are in this next chapter.

Remember, having Autism never means that you will never get to do what you desire in your life. It just means that you need to work extra hard to get what you want exactly. Having Autism just means that you have a steeper hill to climb to the top, which are your desires. You know what I mean!! So find out more how much I have finished climbing my steeper hill that has helped lead me to get to where I'm at today in this next final chapter.

CHAPTER 17: How Grateful I Have Become

n this final chapter of this book, you are now reading how I have reached the top of climbing the steeper hill; you are about to find out how I have proved others who were in charge of me wrong. This chapter will of course show you what it is like to beat any odds when it comes to having Autism. I also wrote this last chapter as a closing to this book, as my own Autism story has come to an end in this chapter. So, with this, there is no need to write a closing chapter such as an Afterword of this book. Enjoy reading the rest of my Autism journey, as you will find out how I really became the person I am today and you will find out more of the milestones I have made that have helped me to become so as well.

I started to get all A's in all of my classes again as I got a Student of the Month during my senior year of high school. It was difficult getting all A's in some of the tough classes I was taking during both sophomore and junior year. I even remember the proud moment when I went to a Student of the Month breakfast with both my dad and his girlfriend at the time named Jen at Woodhaven Country Club in Palm Desert that was hosted by both my high school and the Optimus Club. They would host this every month for one boy and one girl student for each grade from high school. So then, I felt so proud of receiving my Student of the Month certificate before heading on to school, as that has really boosted my day with lots of pride about all the hard work I had done, especially throughout my last great year of high school.

I graduated from Palm Desert High School on June 4th, 2016, with a 3.7 GPA. With this, I felt not only all the proudness that I have finally made it from first grade of being in special ed class to being in all regular classes in high school and then finally graduating with my high school diploma, but I have felt that I have proved those who were in charge of me wrong, along with them stating and thinking that I was never going to make it all the way through grade school and graduate with all As. As this applies to what they told my father on the day of my first IEP meeting that I would never walk that stage and receive my diploma and mainstream that we've all been working on while I was in special ed classes.

Myself and my father Eric Weaver at my high school graduation.

A month later after graduating high school and turning eighteen, I passed and got my personal trainer's certification after I took the test online. With this, this was another proud moment for me as this has also been my dream career starting at eight years old, along with still wanting to become a trainer once Dad asked me if I still want to be a trainer back when I was fourteen before he handed me the manual. This was another accomplishment for me as I really felt official after passing that test as much as I have been shadowing my father on how to train people at his gym called Get-Fit in Palm Desert before I even took the exam. When I also shadowed my father, I even started to feel more positive that this career really fits me, as I have always been interested in fitness along with working out, so why not help others in need with their own fitness goals when they need it? Plus, the career seemed really fun and easy, as my father would even let me train some of his clients at the gym as he would watch and teach me all along as well.

I also started to attend College of the Desert in Palm Desert, California, in the fall right after high school graduation to study for my AA degree in Kinesiology, as this took me four years to study for.

Just a month before I turned nineteen, I passed the driver's test and got my driver's license. As much as I'd been waiting for this day to finally become an official driver on the road, I started to feel even more achieved that I can actually take on any challenge such as learning how to drive and then becoming a driver on the road, regardless of my own Autism. I had been wanting to become more independent on my own, especially when it came to driving, as I had never let my own Autism become my own barrier from achieving my own dreams and goals.

Six months later, as I was nineteen, Dad bought me a black Toyota Tacoma 2012 truck. The day when my father said to me, "We're going to finally buy you a truck," was an amazing surprise day for me as I finally got my own independence of now being able to drive to wherever location I need to take myself. I actually still have lots of the confidence to now be able to take any risks on the road publicly as I have never let my own Autism make it difficult to take any challenge I need to face in the real world.

Austinn Weaver

Myself with my new Toyota Tacoma 2012 truck that my father Eric bought me.

During my second year of attending C.O.D., I got on my first Dean's List for Fall 2017 semester at C.O.D. I didn't even expect that I would still make such an amazing accomplishment like this in college as much as I always look back to what I have achieved all throughout grade school and even high school.

When I was twenty-one, I graduated and got my AA degree in Kinesiology from College of the Desert. With this, I'd been thinking to myself of how far I had gotten throughout my whole academic life with my own Autism, starting from the very beginning of first grade to now. I understand that college can be tougher than high school, especially for those with Autism, as it depends where they're at on the spectrum, but with my own Autism, college was never a problem for me as long as I stayed focused and never gave up on my dream of getting that degree, despite some of the tough courses I was taking due to my major. Just gotta keep pushing through, especially for something that you want bad enough to where you want to work extra

hard for it!!

At home in Palm Desert, California, showing my AA degree in Kinesiology while

in my cap and gown.

Then at age twenty-two, I attended California State University San Bernardino in

the fall of 2020 to study for my B.A. degree in Business Administration -

Entrepreneurship.

Plus, I started to become a part of the Sigma Nu Tau Entrepreneurship Honor

Society during my second semester at CSUSB.

At age twenty-three, Dad and I moved to Prescott Valley, Arizona to be close to

family, such as my mom, grandparents, and all of Mom's side of family, as I continued my schooling online like what I've been doing anyway because of the Covid pandemic during that year of 2020.

Then at age twenty-four, Dad and I opened up Get-Fit Prescott in Prescott, Arizona, as this has been the first business I have ever owned.

(Left) Myself and my father Eric at our gym Get-Fit. (Right) The front view of our gym in Prescott, Arizona.

I started to become a part of the NSLS on February 14, 2023 after I got the email from my college to sign up to become a part of this special program. I started to feel even more special after reading the email that I got accepted into this program because of my high GPA of a 3.583, as my college has recently just started its own chapter for this program just this year of 2023, along with the NSLS program being around since September 2001.

Finally, on May 20, 2023, I graduated with my BA degree in Business Administration - Entrepreneurship from California State University San Bernardino, as I also graduated with Cum Laude Honors because of my high GPA of a 3.5. I also got on the Dean's List five times while attending CSUSB as well during semesters of Fall 2020, Fall 2021, Spring 2022, Fall 2022, and Spring 2023. I have also became the first generation college student within my own family as well.

(From top left to bottom left: Myself with my father Eric, myself with my mother Lisa and stepdad Sean, and myself with both of my grandparents named Tom and Luz at my CSUSB graduation in Ontario, California.)

With this along with my own proud moment of how far I have gone with my own schooling, despite my own Autism, I have become more proud as I started to think back to where I started back in elementary school and being in all special education classes and being told that I would never make it this far and graduate with my peers to now even graduating with honors for the first time. This has come to show to those who have been in charge of me in the past that it is always possible to still achieve your own dreams and goals, even when they never believed and stated that I would never be the person I am today. Same can apply to others who are on the spectrum too to where they can also do anything they wish to do in life as they too need to prove others wrong. Others who may also be in charge of anyone on the spectrum always judged by the outside appearance and not the inside appearance of those on the spectrum; to where those with Autism are also smarter than you can imagine as they also have their own desires and feelings just like other people in life. All others that are not on the spectrum have to do is to always accept those with Autism and believe that they too can achieve anything in life and become their mentor and then it will become a possibility for them to go even farther in life that you've been imagining of as well.

I sometimes would imagine where on the spectrum I would be if I would not have all the support from my father, my mother, and Jessica; and if I would not have someone to believe in me. I am grateful of the person I have become mainly because they all did what was best for me and my own Autism.

All it takes to help your child on the spectrum to become the person that he or she wishes to become is for you to believe in your child as it also mostly takes the time, patience, and the understanding to do so as well. So besides everyone on the spectrum being different, depending on their spectrum level of low, medium, or high functioning, some may take a short period of time as others may take a longer period of time to develop the desired skills. As of course, communication is one of these examples! Understanding and communicating to those who are nonverbal is like learning another language. Even though they cannot speak, they of course can still show emotion, along with using some sign language that show they want or need something. As myself, reaching my arm out and going "UH UH!" at a younger age, like I addressed at the beginning of this book, is an example of this too. So work with your child with developing any skill like speaking, and never give up and lose hope as you do so as, again, all it takes is patience. So depending on your child, who knows if it would take 5 months, a year, 2 years, etc. for your child's skills to develop. Believe in your child, and it is only YOU AND YOUR CHILD who can predict the future and not those who would be in charge of your child by saying it's impossible for your child to do what everyone else does, such as graduating high school, speak, etc.

Remember, EVERYTHING IS POSSIBLE WITH AUTISM, as this is why I wrote this book so you too can know and also believe that desires can still be accomplished, whether it is for your child on the spectrum or even if it is for you who is on the spectrum as well. So whether if it is for your child, yourself on the spectrum, or even if you are just curious how the Autism mind works, just remember that everyone with Autism are unique in their own way, as Autism is never a disability; it is a SUPERPOWER! I hope you believe this as you have already read all of my story throughout this book. I even hoped for those with Autism who do not have the extra support from a loved one and is facing Autism alone have found this book to give them hope as well and that it is possible of course to face the obstacles alone too. Just remember that for yourself without the extra support, never lose hope either and always be proud of the special person you are.

If you also feel that someone else you know, whether it is another parent struggling with helping his or her child with Autism or even if it is someone with Autism who may feel left out from being like everyone else and who needs the extra inspiration and positivity, then feel free to pass this book forward to whoever needs it most. Together, let's keep spreading the word about how special of a gift Autism is and that again, EVERYTHING IS POSSIBLE WITH AUTISM, no matter where on the spectrum you or your child may be and no matter however long it may take for whatever Autism obstacle to be overcome. So, in this way, everyone would have the understanding of Autism awareness and that even everyone else would see the special power within Autism and never again think of it as a DISABILITY. And even they can always keep in mind to accept those with Autism and never isolate them from everyone else. So feel free to pass this book to someone who needs to understand more about Autism as well. As I always say too: AUTISM ROCKS!!

References

LevelAhead ABA. (2025). *Essential Autism Statistics & Facts 2024.*

https://www.levelaheadaba.com/important-autism-statistics-2024#:~:text=According%20

to%20the%20Centers%20for%20Disease%20Control,increase%20of%20178%%20sinc

e%20the%20year%202000.